FIFTY STEPS
IN SIGHT-SINGING

FIFTY STEPS
IN SIGHT-SINGING

by

Arthur Somervell

YESTERDAY'S CLASSICS

ITHACA, NEW YORK

This edition, first published in 2021 by Yesterday's Classics, an imprint of Yesterday's Classics, LLC, is an unabridged republication of the text originally published by J. Curwen & Sons Ltd. For the complete listing of the books that are published by Yesterday's Classics, please visit www.yesterdaysclassics.com. Yesterday's Classics is the publishing arm of Gateway to the Classics which presents the complete text of hundreds of classic books for children at www.gatewaytotheclassics.com.

ISBN: 978-1-63334-152-4

Yesterday's Classics, LLC
PO Box 339
Ithaca, NY 14851

PREFACE

IT is slowly beginning to be recognised that to be unable to read a single line of music at sight is, after all, rather a sign of ignorance. This is encouraging, and should be made the most of by all who have at heart the spread of musical education, and the consequent advancement of music in this country.

In our elementary schools the teaching of sight-reading forms part of the curriculum; and although good results are only obtained in places where enthusiasm backs the requirements of the Board of Education, there is no reason why a much wider and more thorough knowledge of this subject should not be fostered, if teachers could only realise the fact that the teaching of sight-reading is not a subject demanding special artistic gifts, any more than the teaching of reading requires a special knowledge of literature.

But putting aside the elementary schools, where, in many places, excellent work is being done in this direction, if we turn to the secondary schools, it is here that we find the subject, except in a few cases, totally neglected.

In most of them singing is rarely treated *educationally*.[1] The singing-class, where there is one, exists mainly for the practice of music (learned for the most part by ear), for a school entertainment. It is true that the members of the class usually hold the music in their hands; but for all the value it is to them, books of the words would in most cases supply all that is needed.

In boys' preparatory schools the subject is even more generally neglected, with the result that practically no boy who goes on to a public school can read music at all, unless he happens to have picked

---

[1]No subject can be treated educationally in the time usually allowed—from half an hour to one hour per week.

up the barest smattering of the subject by learning an instrument; and even then, unless he is, musically, unusually intelligent, it is of little value to him when he comes to sing a part in a choir. Nor does there seem to be any attempt in these schools to foster a love of or veneration for music.

When the boys pass on to a public school they usually find that the music master is not only a first-rate musician, but an enthusiast. But the work of such a man is greatly hampered by the fact that the large majority of boys come to him, not only ignorant of what music is, but totally unequipped for the study of it. Those who are put into the choir gradually pick up a vague idea of reading; but the time wasted in grinding through and through a piece of music, in order to teach the bare notes, is heart-breaking; while the fact that the boys never learned *when young* to read at sight makes it practically impossible for them ever really to acquire the power to do so.

This is a point which cannot be urged too strongly upon parents and teachers; for experience shows that the younger a child is (within reason) when he begins to learn sight-reading the more easily will he master the subject. I have often heard whole classes of children under six years old singing from the staff in the key of C; and I know one school in West Norfolk where every child over twelve years old can sing almost anything at sight, because they have been properly taught from infancy. The time given to music in this school is ten minutes a day.

Many parents are now beginning to see the folly of allowing the younger generation to grow up ignorant of a subject so easily taught in childhood, and are asking that this state of things, at least as regards their own children, shall cease to exist. And so numerous have been the enquiries from different sources for a book which will be a guide in working out a scheme of sight-reading lessons that I am, to a certain extent, trying to meet this demand by publishing some of the results of my own experiences with a class of small children.

Teachers must use their own discretion as to when to go on from one lesson to the next, for, in the case of some children, the same lesson may have to be worked through several times, and frequent recapitulation of back work will be found advisable. A short time (say fifteen minutes) spent on these lessons every day will be found more valuable than a longer time once or twice a week.

The important question of the training of the child-voice, the learning of songs, and the class of music to be learned have not been touched upon; but with regard to the last, it should be remembered that to teach a child, or perform for his "delectation," a piece of bad music, is as unpardonable as to recommend *"Scraps"* as an example of literary art. It is unfair to make anyone grind at a subject such as sight-reading, without at the same time giving some idea of what the drudgery will eventually lead to; therefore it behoves parents to see that their children are introduced to a good class of music alongside the sight-reading lessons; exactly as most children learn poetry and have stories read to them while they are learning to read.

It is commonly asserted that "good" music is difficult, and that herein lies the impossibility of giving children any knowledge of it in families where no one plays the piano well. But there is a huge storehouse of good music, classical in every sense of the word, which is not only not difficult, but, on the contrary, delightfully easy to learn—the traditional songs of England, Scotland, Wales, and Ireland. These can be learned and sung (many would say with advantage) without pianoforte accompaniment; and it is hardly necessary to point out that children have a right to this great national and natural heritage. Those who have never tried to teach these songs will be astonished at the ease and pleasure with which children pick them up; and there is no doubt that a large acquaintance with them forms the best and most normal foundation upon which to build, in later life, a knowledge and appreciation of music in its greatest forms.

NOTE TO THIRD EDITION.—The attention of teachers is particularly called to the three Appendices at the end of the book.

ARTHUR SOMERVELL

KENSINGTON, 1904.

APPARATUS

(i) A pointer or small baton.

(ii) A Tonic Sol-fa Modulator (seven keys).

(iii) A blackboard, blank on one side and ruled for music on the other.

(iv) A note-book for each child.

(v) An MS. music-book for each child.

THE STAFF MODULATOR

A stave should be drawn upon the blackboard with lines about three inches apart whenever a new key is being first explained. It is not necessary to write in more than the chord of the Key.

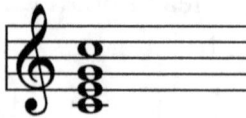 or

FIFTY STEPS IN SIGHT-SINGING

STEP I (Sol-fa)

(i) The class should learn the mental effect of *doh soh doh*[1] and afterwards the *me* may be added. The hand-signs should also be taught, and the class learn to sing these notes in any order, the teacher either pointing to the notes on the modulator or giving the hand-signs.

(ii) The following or similar passages should be written on the blackboard and sung slowly by the class.

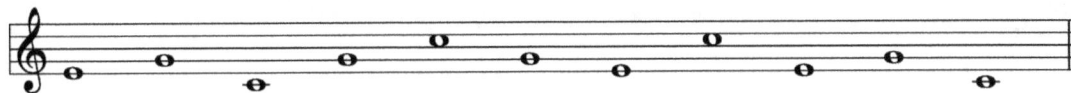

Example:—

d m d s m d d¹ s d¹ s m s d s d¹ s m d¹ m s d

(iii) *Ear-tests.*—One of the four notes should be sung by the teacher to the syllable *laa*, and the class, or individual children, should then sing any one of the other three asked for. This is a most useful exercise.

STEP II (Staff)

(i) A short recapitulation of the first part of Step I.

(ii) A large stave should be drawn on the blackboard, and middle C written in and called *doh*. The class should then count the scale degrees on the Tonic Sol-fa Modulator from *doh* to *doh*[1], and then the lines and spaces on the stave from middle C upwards. The place of *doh*[1] can thus be found, and in the same way the places of *me* and *soh*. The class should then (using the Sol-fa names) sing these notes in any order as the teacher points to them on the Staff Modulator.

(iii) The following or similar passages should be written on the blackboard and sung slowly by the class:—

(iv) *Ear-tests.*—The teacher should sing very slowly a passage formed from these notes, *using the Sol-fa names*, and the children must write them down in the staff notation in their MS. books. Afterwards a similar passage should be sung slowly to the syllable *laa* and taken down by the children. It will be found advisable to sing the *doh* between every two notes.

STEP III (SOL-FA)

(i) The class should learn the mental effect of *ray* and *te*, and should sing from pointing on the modulator, as well as from hand-signs, passages introducing the six notes already learned. *Ray* and *te* should not at first be taken by skip (*e.g.*, *soh ray, soh te*, or *me te*).

(ii) The following or similar passages introducing the new notes should be written on the blackboard, and sung slowly by the class:—

Example:—

d r m s m r d s d¹ t d¹ s m r m s d¹ t d¹ s m r d

(iii) The following or similar ear-tests should be given for the class to write down in their note-books. The chord of the key must be played or sung between each test, and each test given twice.

Examples:—

d r   d m   m r   m s   d¹ t   s m &c.

STEP IV (STAFF)

(i) A short recapitulation of the first part of Step III.

(ii) The staff modulator having been drawn on the blackboard and the chord of C written in, the places of *ray* and *te* may easily be found by the children by reference to the Sol-fa modulator. When found, these may be written on the blackboard as small opaque notes to the right of the chord.

The class should then sing the notes already learned as the teacher points to them.

(iii) The following or similar passages should be written on the blackboard and sung slowly by the children.

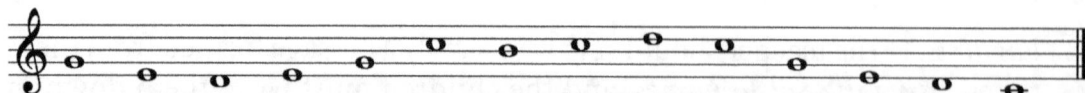

(iv) *Ear-tests.*—The chord of the key having been sung or played the teacher should sing to the syllable *laa* any two of the notes already learned, and the children should write them down in the staff notation in their MS. books.

STEP V (Sol-fa)

(i) The class should learn the mental effect of *fah* and *lah*, and should sing from pointing on the modulator, as well as from hand-signs, passages introducing all the notes of the octave. *Fah* and *lah* should not at first be taken by skip (*e.g.,* r f f r f l m l d¹ l &c.)

(ii) The following or similar passages, introducing the new notes, should be written on the blackboard, and sung slowly by the class.

Example:—

d r m r m s f m r d d¹ t l t d¹ s l s f m s l t d¹ s f m r d

(iii) The following or similar ear-tests should be sung to the syllable *laa* (or played) for the class to write down in their note-books. The chord of the key must be played or sung between each test, and each test given twice.

Example:—

s f m f s l d¹ t &c.

STEP VI (Staff)

(i) A short recapitulation of the first part of Step V.

(ii) The Staff Modulator having been drawn on the blackboard with the six notes already learned, the places of *fah* and *lah* may easily be found by the children by reference to the Sol-fa Modulator. When found, these may be written on the blackboard as small opaque notes to the right of the chord of C.

The class should then sing the notes already learned as the teacher points to them.

(iii) The following or similar passages should be written on the blackboard, and sung slowly by the children.

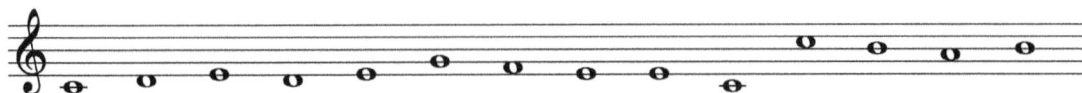

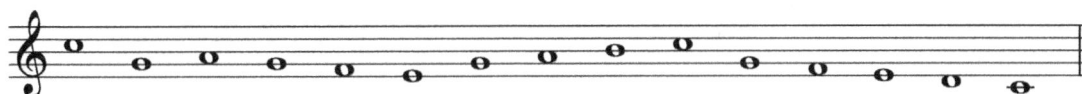

(iv) *Ear-tests.*—The chord of the key having been sung or played, the teacher should sing to the syllable *laa* any two of the notes already learned, and the children should write them down in the staff notation in their MS. books.

STEP VII (Sol-fa)

(i) Practice on the modulator.[2]

(ii) Two-beat measure should be explained to the class, and examples of well-known tunes in this time sung, both teacher and class beating time.

(iii) The following or similar time tests should be written on the blackboard and sung first to the time-names[3] and afterwards to the syllable *doh* or *lah* (in some ways *doh* is better than *lah*, as it is an easier sound to articulate sharply:—

{| d :— | d :— | d :d | d :d | d :— | d :d | d :d | d :— ||

(iv) Exercises 1, 3, 4, 5, 6, and 7 in the "Criterion Sight-reader" (Part I) should be sung, with teacher and class beating time:—

KEY **G.**

{| d :m | s :f | m :r | f :m | r :m | d :r | t₁ :l₁ | s₁ :— }

{| s :f | m :r | d :t₁ | r :d | l₁ :t₁ | d :s | f :r | d :— ||

KEY **F.**

{| m :f | l :s | f :m | r :d | r :m | s :f | m :r | m :— }

{| d :r | f :m | r :m | s :f | m :f | l :s | f :r | d :— ||

KEY **E♭.**

{| d¹ :s | m :f | s :d | m :r | t₁ :d | r :m | f :m | f :— }

{| m :f | l :s | f :s | t :l | d¹ :s | m :f | m :r | d :— ||

[2]Each lesson should now begin with a short practice on the Sol-fa or Staff Modulator, according to the notation in use at the lesson, when the more difficult intervals may be gradually mastered.

[3]See Appendix II.

KEY **C.**

s :s |d' :d |r :m |f :l |s :d |s :f |m :f |r :—

r :m |f :l |m :f |s :d' |s :s |d' :d |r :m |d :—

KEY **D.**

d :m |s :f |m :r |d :— |m :s |d' :l |s :f |m :—

s :m |d :r |m :f |s :— |d' :s |m :f |m :r |d :—

KEY **F.**

d :t, |d :r |m :f |m :— |s :l |s :f |m :f |r :—

m :f |m :r |d :m |s :— |s :l |s :d |r :m |d :—

(v) Ear-tests of two notes (as in Step V) should be sung or played and written down by the children in their note-books.

STEP VIII (Staff)

(i) Practice on the modulator.

(ii) $\frac{2}{2}$ and $\frac{2}{4}$ time should be explained to the class and examples of well-known tunes in this time (simple duple) again sung, both teacher and class beating time.

(iii) The following or similar time-tests should be written on the blackboard, and sung first to the time-names[4] and afterwards to the syllable *doh*.

[4]See Appendix II.

(iii) The following or similar exercises should be written on the blackboard, and sung slowly by the class.

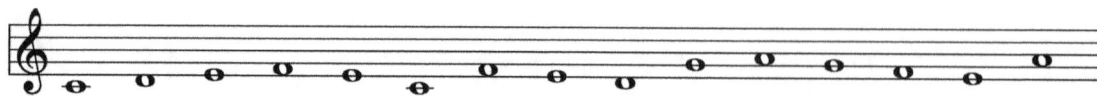

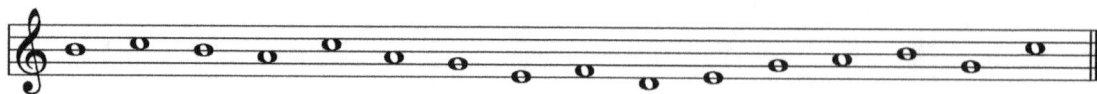

(iv) Ear-tests of two notes should be taken down by the class in the staff notation.

STEP IX (SOL-FA)

(i) Practice on the modulator.

(ii) A simple piece of two-beat rhythm should be written on the blackboard, and sung by the children:—

Example:—

{| d :— | d :d | d :d | d :— | d :d | d :d | d :d | d :— }

{| d :d | d :d | d :d | d :d | d :— | d :— | d :— | — :— ||

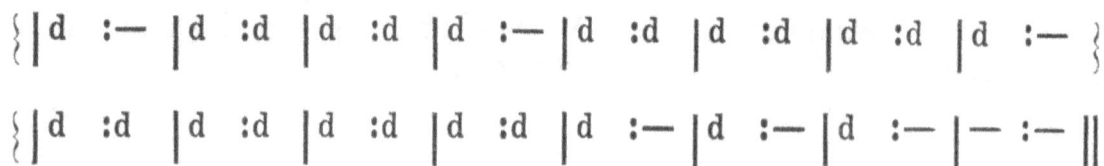

followed by a passage in tune only:—

Example:—

d m s f m r r m f l s f m d' t l t d' s l s f r d

When these have been read through a few times, they should be combined:—

Example:—

{| d :— | m :s | f :m | r :— | r :m | f :l | s :f | m :— }

{| d' :t | l :t | d' :s | l :f | m :— | r :— | d :— | — :— ||

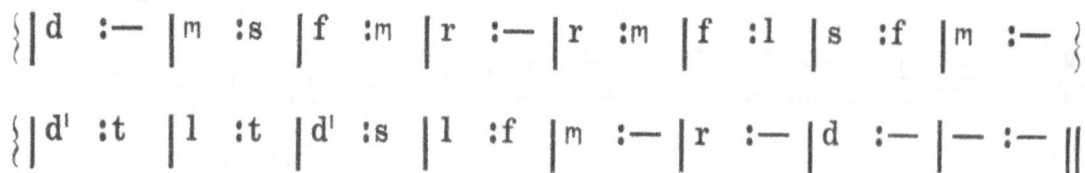

(iii) As the children improve in writing the ear-tests correctly the difficulty may be increased, occasionally tests of three notes being given.

Example:—

d m r   s l s   d' t l   m s f &c.

STEP X (STAFF)

(i) Practice on the modulator.

(ii) A simple piece of $\frac{2}{4}$ rhythm should be written on the blackboard, and sung by the class first to the time-names and afterwards to the syllable *doh*.

Example:—

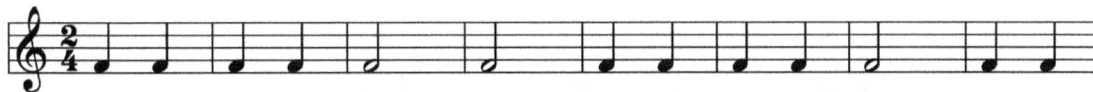

Then a passage in tune only:—

Example:—

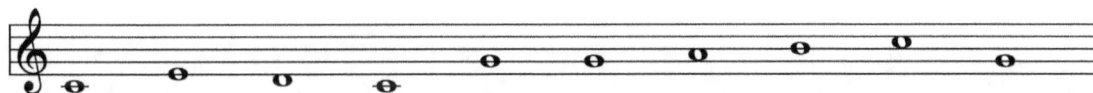

When these have been read a few times, they should be combined:—

Example:—

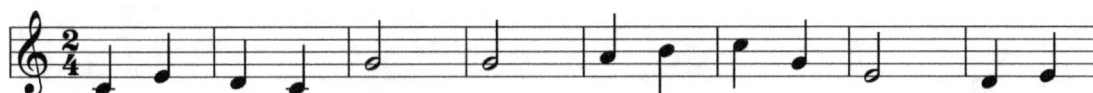

(iii) Rather more difficult ear-tests may be given for the class to write down in the staff notation in their MS. books.

STEP XI (SOL-FA)

(i) Practice on the modulator, introducing the notes *fe* and *ta*.

(ii) The following or similar exercises to be written on the blackboard, and sung slowly by the class.

Example:—

d   m   s   fe s   m   f   r   d   s   fe s   d¹   ta   l   t   d¹

s   fe s   l   t   d¹   ta   l   s   l   t   d¹   s   fe s   d

(iii) Exercises 26 to 32 in the "Criterion Sight Reader," Part I:—

KEY **G.**

| m :r.m | r :d.r | d :t₁ | t₁ :d | r :d.t₁ | l₁ :d | t₁ :— | — :s₁ |

| m :r.m | f :m | l₁ :— | — :l₁ | r :d.r | m :r | s₁ :— | — :s₁ |

| s₁ :s₁.s₁ | s₁ :s₁.s₁ | s₁ :s₁ | s₁ :s₁ | m :r.m | r :d.r | d :t₁ | t₁ :s₁ |

| f :m.f | m :r | s :— | — :s₁.l₁ | t₁ :s₁ | — :l₁.t₁ | d :l₁ | — :t₁.d |

| r :t₁ | — :d.r | m :r.m | r :d.r | d :t₁ | t₁ :m | r :-.s₁ | s₁ :r |

| d :-.l₁ | l₁ :f | m :s₁ | s₁ :s₁ | s₁ :s₁ | l₁.t₁:d.r | m :r.m | r :d.r |

| d :t₁ | t₁.d:r.m | f.f:f | : | m.m:m | : | r :s | r :s |

| r :s₁ | r :s₁ | s₁ :s₁ | s₁ :s₁ | d.d:d | : ‖

KEY **A.**

| m :s₁.l₁ | s₁ :s₁.l₁ | s₁ :d | d :r.m | f : | f : | f :— | — :f₁ |

| m₁ : | m₁ : | m :s₁.l₁ | s₁ :s₁.l₁ | s₁ :d | d :-.t₁ | l₁ : | d : |

| s₁ : | :s₁ | l₁ :s₁.l₁ | t₁ :l₁.t₁ | d :t₁.d | r :d.r | m :s₁.l₁ | s₁ :s₁.l₁ |

| s₁ :d | d : | l₁ :r | r : | t₁ :m | m :m | m :s₁.l₁ | s₁ :s₁.l₁ | s₁ :d | d : |

| t₁ : | l₁ : | s₁ :-.s₁ | s₁ :-.s₁ | s₁ :s₁ | s₁ :s₁ | s₁ :s₁ | l₁.t₁:d.r |

| m :s₁.l₁ | s₁ :s₁.l₁ | s₁ :d | d.r:m.f | m : | r : | d : | : ‖

KEY **D**.

{ :d | d :r.m|f :m | l :l | s :d¹ | r :-.m|s :f | m :— |— :f }

{ | s :d | d¹ :-.t| l :d¹ | s :f.m|r.m:f | m :-.r| d :— |— ‖ }

KEY **B♭**.

{ | s₁ :m₁.f₁| s₁.f₁:m₁ | f₁ :r₁.m₁| f₁ :— | s₁.s₁:m₁ | f₁.f₁:r₁ | m₁.m₁:r₁ | r₁ :— }

{ | m₁.f₁:s₁ | l₁.t₁:d | t₁.d:r | r :— | m :r.d | t₁.d:r.d | t₁.t₁:l₁ | s₁ :— }

{ | s₁.s₁:s₁ | s₁.s₁:s₁ | s₁ :l₁.l₁| s₁ : | l₁.l₁:l₁ | l₁.l₁:l₁ | r.r :r | r :— }

{ | d :d.d | t₁.t₁:t₁ | l₁ :l₁.l₁| s₁ :— | f₁ :s₁.l₁| s₁.l₁:t₁.d| r :t₁ | d :— ‖ }

KEY **D**.

{ | d¹ :d | d :d | d.r:m.f|m.r:d | r :r | r :r.m| f :s | m :— }

{ | m :-.d f :-.r | s :-.m|l :-.f| t :-.s|t :-.s| d¹ :d | d :d }

{ | d.r:m.f| : | : |m.r:d | m.r:d | d :-.m| r :-.f|m :-.s }

{ | f :-.l|s :-.t| l :-.d¹|t :-.r¹|d¹ :d | d :d | d.r:m | : }

{ | f.s:l | : | s.l:t | : | d¹ :— |— :— ‖ }

KEY **D**.

{ :m.f| s.l:s.l | s.l:s.f | m.f:m.r | d :r | m.r:d.r|m.f:s.l | l :— | r :m.f }

{ | s.l:s.l | s :m.f| s.l:s.l | s :l.t | d¹.t:d¹.l | s.m:d.f | r :— | d ‖ }

KEY **G**.

{ | d.s₁:d.r | m :r.d | s :-.s| s :— | f.s:f.m | r :— | m.f:m.r | d :— }

{ | d.s₁:d.r | m :r.d| f :f | f :— | m.s:d.m | s₁.d:m.s | m :r | d :— }

{ | t₁ :l₁.t₁| d.r:m | r :-.r | r :— | d :t₁.d| r.m:f | m :m | m : }

{ | s.m:d.s₁| d.r:m | f.r:t₁.s₁| t₁.r:f | m :s₁ | m :s₁ | m :r | d :— }

{ | d :— | d :-.d| d :— | :d.d| d :d |— :d | d :— | d : ‖ }

(iv) Ear-tests to include *fe* and *ta* only when taken stepwise (*e.g.*, **s fe s, d' ta l**).

STEP XII (STAFF)

(i) Practice on the modulator, introducing the sharpened 4th and flattened 7th of the scale. Perpendicular lines should be drawn on each side of the chord of the key, the F being sharpened to the right and the B flattened to the left of the lines. In pointing for the class F to the right of the right hand line is always F♯ *(fe)*, B to the left of the left hand line is always B♭ *(ta)*.

(ii) The following or similar exercises should be written on the blackboard, and sung slowly by the class.

Example:—

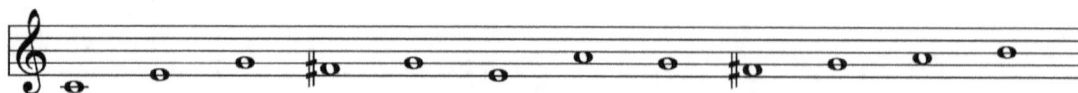

(iii) Easy exercises in Time and Tune:—

(iv) Ear-tests introducing F# and B♭ only when taken stepwise, *e.g.*:—

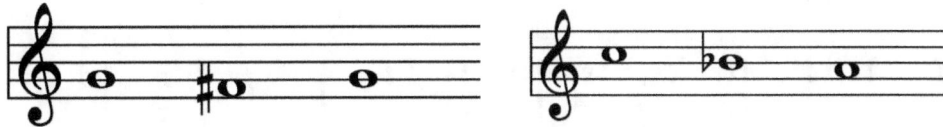

STEP XIII (SOL-FA)

(i) The class should now learn to sing from the modulator, in the open key, using the syllable *laa* instead of the Sol-fa names. Practice must be slow at first to ensure the realisation of the mental effect of each note before it is sung.

(ii) The following or similar exercises should be written on the blackboard, and sung to the syllable *laa*.

Example:—

d   m   s   m   r   m   f   s   l   t   d¹   s   l   s   f   m

r   r   s   f   m   s   l   t   d¹   s   l   d¹   m   r   d

(iii) A few easy exercises from the "Criterion Sight Reader" (Part I, Ex. 16-23) sung to *laa*:—

KEY **B♭**.

‖ s₁ :l₁ :t₁ | d :— :t₁ | l₁ :— :t₁ | s₁ :— :— | s₁ :f₁ :m₁ ⟩

‖ r₁ :— :f₁ | m₁ :— :r₁ | d₁ :— :— | d :— :— | d₁ :— :— ‖

KEY **G**.

‖ d :— | d :— | d :— |— :— | r :d | m :r | d :— |— :— ⟩

‖ s :— | s :— | s :— |— :— | f :m | r :f | m :— |— :— ‖

KEY **F.**

$\{\|$ m :m $\|$ s :— $\|$ d :d $\|$ m :— $\|$ f :m $\|$ r :m $\|$ f :l $\|$ s :— $\}$

$\{\|$ s :s $\|$ f :— $\|$ m :m $\|$ r :— $\|$ d :s, $\|$ l, :t, $\|$ d :d $\|$ d :— $\|\|$

KEY **A♭.**

$\{\|$:d $\|$ r :s, :r $\|$ m :— :d $\|$ m :s, :m $\|$ f :— :f $\|$ s :s, :s $\}$

$\{\|$ f :l, :f $\|$ m :s, :r $\|$ m :— :— $\|$ m :s, :r $\|$ d :— $\|\|$

KEY **G.**

$\{\|$ s :f :r $\|$ f :m :d $\|$ m :r :l, $\|$ t, :— :d $\|$ r :m :f $\}$

$\{\|$ s, :l, :t, $\|$ d :s :f $\|$ r :— :— $\|$ d :m :r $\|$ d :— :— $\|\|$

KEY **E.**

$\{\|$ d :— $\|$ t, :d $\|$ r :— $\|$ d :r $\|$ m :r $\|$ d :m $\|$ r :— $\|$— :— $\}$

$\{\|$ m :— $\|$ r :m $\|$ f :— $\|$ m :f $\|$ s :f $\|$ r :t, $\|$ d :— $\|$— :— $\|\|$

KEY **C.**

$\{\|$ d' :d' $\|$ s :s $\|$ m :m $\|$ d :d $\|$ r :r $\|$ m :f $\|$ s :l $\|$ s :— $\}$

$\{\|$ d' :d' $\|$ s :s $\|$ m :m $\|$ d :d $\|$ r :m $\|$ f :s $\|$ l :s $\|$ d :— $\|\|$

KEY **C.**

$\{\|$ d :m $\|$ s :f $\|$ l :s $\|$ t :l $\|$ d' :t $\|$ s :l $\|$ f :s $\|$ m :— $\}$

$\{\|$ m :s $\|$ d' :t $\|$ r' :d' $\|$ l :t $\|$ s :l $\|$ f :s $\|$ m :r $\|$ d :— $\|\|$

(iv) *Ear-tests.*—From this point the tests should always comprise three notes.

STEP XIV (STAFF)

(i) The class should learn to sing from the Staff modulator in the key of C, using the syllable *laa* instead of the Sol-fa names. Practice at first must be slow.

(ii) The following or similar exercises should be written on the blackboard, and sung slowly by the children to the syllable *laa*.

Example:—

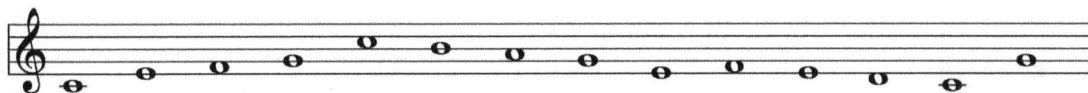

(iii) A few exercises in Time and Tune sung to *laa*:—

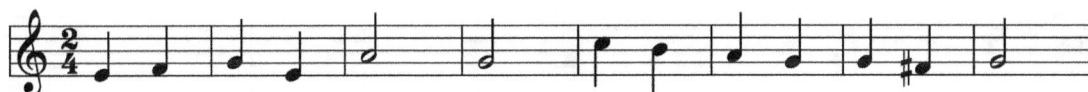

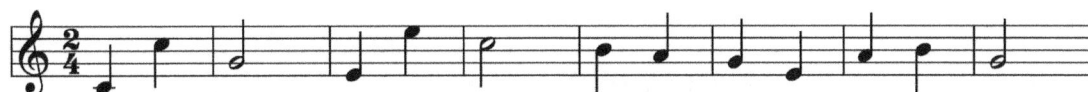

(iv) Ear-tests of three notes.

STEP XV (SOL-FA)

(i) Practice on the modulator (Sol-fa).

(ii) Three-beat measure and $\frac{3}{4}$ time (staff notation) should be explained to the class, and well-known tunes in triple time sung, both teacher and children beating time (*down, right, up*).

(iii) The following or similar tests to be written on the blackboard, and sung by the class to the time-names and afterwards to the syllable *doh*.

Examples:—

(iv) *(a)* Exercises in Time and Tune; 59, 63, and 65 in the "Criterion Sight Reader," Part I:—

KEY **G.**

{| m :f :s | m :s₁ :m | r :l :s | r :m :f | t₁ :d :r | l₁ :t₁ :d }

{| s₁ :f :m | r :— :— | s :f :m | l₁ :t₁ :d | l :s :f | t₁ :d :r }

{| m :l₁ :f | m :s₁ :m | r :— :— | l₁ :— :r | d :— :— | d :— :— ||

(b) Exercises in Time and Tune:—

(v) The use and value of a dot should be explained to the class, and passages on one note introducing dotted minims written on the blackboard, and sung by the children. (The time-names should be used.)

STEP XVI (SOL-FA AND STAFF)

(i) Practice on the Staff Modulator.

(ii) Four-beat measure and $\frac{4}{4}$ time (staff notation) should be explained to the class, and well-known tunes in quadruple time sung, both teacher and children beating time (*down, left, right, up*).

(iii) The following or similar tests to be written on the blackboard, and sung by the class first to the time-names and afterwards to the syllable *doh*.

Examples:—

$$\{ | \text{d} : \text{d} | \text{d} : \text{d} | \text{d} :- | \text{d} :- | \text{d} : \text{d} | \text{d} :- | \text{d} : \text{d} | \text{d} :- \}$$

$$\{ | \text{d} :- | \text{d} : \text{d} | \text{d} :- | \text{d} : \text{d} | \text{d} : \text{d} | \text{d} : \text{d} | \text{d} :- | - :- \|$$

(iv) *(a)* Exercises in Sol-fa ("Criterion Music Reader," Part I, Ex. 49, 50, 53, 55):—

KEY **D.**

$\{|$ d :d $|$ s :— $|$ m :m $|$ d' :— $|$ t :s $|$ f :l $|$ s :— $|$ m :— $\}$

$\{|$ f :m $|$ r :— $|$ s :f $|$ m :— $|$ d' :— $|$ s :m $|$ r :— $|$ d :— $\|$

KEY **D.**

$\{|$ d :— $|$— :— $|$ r :— $|$— :— $|$ m :— $|$— :— $|$ d :— $|$— :— $\}$

$\{|$ d :— $|$ r :— $|$ m :— $|$ d :— $|$ d :r $|$ m :d $|$ m :d $|$ m :— $\}$

$\{|$ m :f $|$ s :— $|$ m :s $|$ d' :— $|$ m :— $|$ f :— $|$ s :— $|$— :— $\}$

$\{|$ m :— $|$ s :— $|$ d' :— $|$— :— $|$ m :— $|$— :— $|$ s :— $|$— :— $\}$

$\{|$ d' :— $|$— :— $|$ d :— $|$— :— $\|$

KEY **D.**

$\{|$ d :— $|$ m :m $|$ s :s $|$ d' :— $|$ s :s $|$ d :— $|$ s :— $|$ d :— $\}$

$\{|$ d :— $|$— :— $|$ d :— $|$— :— $|$ d :— $|$ d :— $|$ d :— $|$— :— $\}$

$\{|$ d :— $|$— :— $|$ d :— $|$ d :— $|$ d :d' $|$— :— $\|$

KEY **D.**

$\{$:d $|$ m : $|$:r $|$ d : $|$:m $|$ s : $|$:f $|$ m : $|$:s $\}$

$\{|$ l :d' $|$ s :m $|$ d : $|$ f : $|$ r : $|$ d :r $|$ m : $|$ s : $\}$

$\{|$ d' : $|$ d : $|$ d : $|$:s $|$ d' : $|$:d $|$ d : $|$:m $\}$

$\{|$ s :d' $|$ s :m $|$ d :m $|$ s :m $|$ d : $|$ d' : $|$ d :— $|$— $\|$

(b) Exercises in Staff:—

(v) The use of the dot should be again explained to the class, and passages on one note, introducing the dotted minim written on the blackboard in $\frac{4}{4}$ time, should be sung by the children.

STEP XVII (SOL-FA)

(i) The class should now be taught the first key remove by practice on the modulator.

(ii) The following or similar exercises, in tune only, should be written on the blackboard, and sung slowly.

Examples:—

KEY **C.**   **G** t.   f.**C.**
d m f s l s ˢd r m f s m d ᵈs l t dˡ s f r m

G t.   f.**C.**
ᵐlₗ tₗ d r m s d ᵈs dˡ mˡ rˡ t dˡ ta l t dˡ m f r d

(iii) Ear-tests containing more difficult intervals (**s l m t d¹ f**).

Examples:—

KEY **D**.

d¹ m r   d¹ f m   s d l   f m t   t d¹ s   l d¹ r

KEY **G**.

d s₁ f   d f t₁   d l₁ m   d r s₁   f r t₁   s₁ f m

STEP XVIII (STAFF)

(i) The Staff Modulator should now be extended to the right so as to include the key of G.

Explain the formation of the scale, showing why F becomes F♯ in the new key. Practise transitions from C to G and *vice versa*. Only the notes of the chord of G should be taught at first.

(ii) The following and similar exercises, in tune only, should be written on the blackboard, and sung slowly by the class to the Sol-fa names.

(iii) Exercises in Time and Tune in G major.

(iv) Ear-tests as in the previous Step.

STEP XIX (Sol-fa)

(i) Recapitulation of Step XVII (i). Modulator practice may include transition to the first key remove by easy skip.

(ii) The following and similar exercises should be written on the blackboard, and sung slowly by the class:—

Example:—

KEY **C.** **G.**t. f.**C.** **G.**t.

d ᵐr r s l s ˢd f m r t, ᵈs d m f s ᵐl, t, d r m

f.**C.**

f s l s f m ᵐt d¹ s l s f l s fe s m f t, d

(iii) Exercises in Bridge-notes, 14, 15, 16, 17 in the "Criterion Sight Reader," Part IV.

KEY **G.** M. 132

{ | s :m | r :d | t, :— | l, :— | s :m | r :ᵈs | f :— | — :— }

{ |ᵐl, :t, | d :r |ᵐl :t | d¹ :d | m :— | r :— | d :— | — :— }

{ | d¹ :— | t :t | d¹s :— | — :— | m :— | f :f | m :— | — :— }

{ | m :r | r :ᵈs | f :f | m :s | ¹r :f | m :r | d :— | — :— ‖

KEY **F**. M. 160.

$\{$ | s :— :m | r :— :d | m :— :d | t₁ :— :l₁ | t₁ :d :r | ˢᵢr₁ :m₁ :f₁ $\}$

$\{$ | m₁ :— :r₁ | d₁ :— :— | ʳᵢs₁ :— :l₁ | t₁ :— :d | l₁ :t₁ :d | m :— :r $\}$

$\{$ | d :t₁ :ᵈs₁ | f₁ :ᵐᵢl₁ :t₁ | d :r :m | r :— :— | s :— :m | r :— :d $\}$

$\{$ | ᵐt₁ :l₁ :s₁ | f₁ :— :ᵐᵢl₁ | t₁ :d :r | ᵐl :t :dᵈ | ᶦm :— :r | d :— :— ‖

KEY **G**. M. 152.

$\{$ .s₁:l₁.s₁ | d :d | d :d | d :— | —.s₁:l₁.s₁ | t₁ :t₁ | t₁ :t₁ $\}$

$\{$ | t₁ :— | .s₁:l₁.s₁ | ᵗᵃᵢf :f | f :f | f :f | s :f $\}$

$\{$ | m :— | m :— | m :— | —.ʳs₁:l₁.s₁ | f :f | f :f $\}$

$\{$ | f :f | s :f | m :— | m :— | m :— | —.s₁:l₁.s₁ $\}$

$\{$ | r :— | s :— | r :— | s :— | d :— | d :— | d :— | —. ‖

KEY **G**. M. 138.

$\{$ | s :— | r :f | m :— | — :— | ᵈs :— | r :f | ᵐl₁ :— | — :— $\}$

$\{$ | t₁ :t₁ | ᵈs :— | f :f | ᵐl₁ :— | t₁ :d | r :f | m :— | — :— $\}$

$\{$ | ᵐl :— | s :t | ᵈᶦs :— | — :— | f :— | s₁ :f | m :— | — :— $\}$

$\{$ | s :r | f :m | ᵈs :r | f :m | ᶠet₁:r | l₁ :t₁ | d :— | — :— ‖

(iv) An easy piece of rhythm should be played or sung two or three times, and the children should write it down in their note-books. The teacher should tell the class in what pulse-measure the test will be, and the books should be barred beforehand.

Example:—

$\{$ | d :— | d :— | d :d | d :— ‖

STEP XX (STAFF)

(i) Modulator practice in the key of G, including all the notes of the scale.

(ii) The following and similar exercises should be written on the blackboard, and sung slowly by the class, to the Sol-fa names.

Example:—

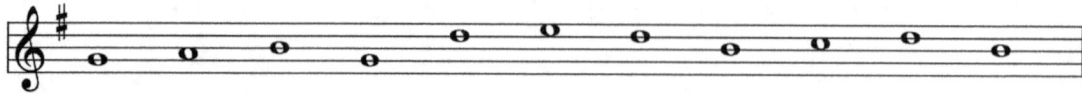

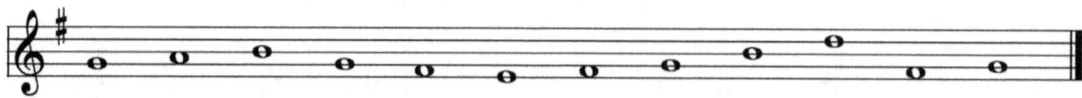

(iii) Exercises in Time and Tune.

(iv) An easy piece of rhythm should be sung or played two or three times, and the children must write it down in the staff notation in their MS. books. The teacher should tell the class in what time the test will be, and the bars should be ready beforehand.

Example:—

STEP XXI (Sol-fa)

(i) Modulator practice should include transition to the first flat key remove.

(ii) The following and similar passages should be written on the blackboard, and sung slowly by the class:—

Example:—

KEY **C.**   f.**F.**   **C**.t.
d m r s d¹ t l s f m ᵐt₁ d r m d s l s ˢd¹ t s l m r d

(iii) An easy piece of rhythm should be played or sung two or three times, and written down by the class in their note-books.

STEP XXII (STAFF)[5]

(i) The Staff Modulator should now be extended to the left so as to include the key of F.

(ii) Explain the formation of the scale, showing why B becomes B♭ in the new key. Only the notes of the chord of F should be taught at first. The children should now evolve for themselves the important rule that when *doh* is a line the *me* and *soh* are the next lines above, the upper *doh* being a space, and *vice versa*. Modulator practice in C and F.

(ii) The following or similar exercises, in tune only, should be written on the blackboard, and sung slowly by the class to the Sol-fa names.

Example:—

(iii) Exercises in Time and Tune.

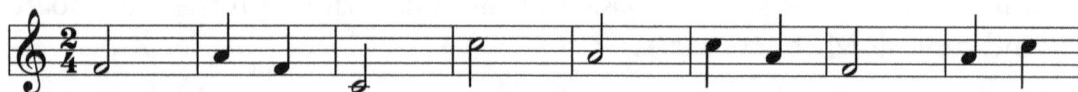

(iv) An easy piece of rhythm should be played or sung two or three times, and written down by the children in the staff notation.

STEP XXIII (Sol-fa)

(i) Modulator practice in three keys.

(ii) The following or similar passages should be written on the blackboard, and sung slowly by the class:—

Example:—

KEY **C.**   **G**.t.   f.**C.**

d   r   m   d   ˢd   r   t₁   d   s   l   s   f   m   ᵐt   d'   s   l

f.**F.**   **C**.t.

d's   l   m   f   l   t   s   m   r   ᵐl   t   d'   f   m   r   d

(iii) Exercises in Time and Tune (36, 37, and 38 in the "Criterion Sight Reader," Part IV).

KEY **F.** M. 152.

{ :m | f :l :f | m :s :m | r :m :d | t₁ :l₁ :s₁ | l₁ :t₁ :ᵈs₁ }

{ | f₁ :— :ᵐl₁ | t₁ :d :r | t₁ :— :r.m | f :l :f | m :s :ᵐl }

{ | t :r' :t | ᵈs :— :f | m :l₁ :f | m :s₁ :r | r :d :t₁ }

{ | d :—:s | ˢd' :r' :t | d' :s :t | d' :f :t | d' :m :t | d' :r' :t }

{ | ᵈs :f :m | r :m :d | t₁ :— :s₁ | ˢr₁ :m₁ :f₁ | f₁ :— :m₁ }

{ | ᵐl₁ :t₁ :d | d :t₁ :d | r :m :f | f :m :r | d :r :t₁ | d :— ||

KEY **D**. M. 160.

$\{|$ d :— :d $|$ r :— :m $|$ f :s :f $|$ m :— :— $|^{f}$d :— :d $|$ r :— :m $\}$

$\{|$ f :s :f $|$ m :— :— $|^{m}$l :t :d^{l} $|$ t :— :s $|^{m}$l$_{\prime}$:t$_{\prime}$:d $|$ t$_{\prime}$:— :l$_{\prime}$ $\}$

$\{|^{s}{}_{\prime}$r :r :m $|$ f :— :— $|^{f}$d :r :m $|$ f :— :— $|$ m :— :— $\}$

$\{|^{m}$l :— :— $|$ t :l :t $|$ d^{l} :— :— $|$ m :— :— $|^{m}$l$_{\prime}$:— :— $\}$

$\{|$ t$_{\prime}$:l$_{\prime}$:t$_{\prime}$ $|$ d :— :— $|^{f}$d^{l} :— :d^{l} $|$ t :l :^{s}r $|$ f :— :f $\}$

$\{|$ m :r :d $|^{r}$s :— :s $|$ f :m :r $|$ m :— :r $|$ d :— :— $\|$

KEY **G**. M. 160.

$\{|$ d :— $|$r :m $|$ t$_{\prime}$:— $|$d :— $|$ l$_{\prime}$:— $|$t$_{\prime}$:d $|$ s$_{\prime}$:— $|$— :— $\}$

$\{|^{s}{}_{\prime}$d :— $|$r :m $|$ t$_{\prime}$:— $|$d :— $|$ r :— $|$m :f $|$ s :— $|$— :— $\}$

$\{|$ s :— $|$l :t $|^{d^{l}}$s :— $|$d :— $|$ l$_{\prime}$:— $|$t$_{\prime}$:d $|$ r :— $|$— :— $\}$

$\{|^{s}$d^{l} :t $|$d^{l} :l $|^{s}$d :t$_{\prime}$ $|$d :l$_{\prime}$ $|$ s$_{\prime}$:— $|$t$_{\prime}$:— $|$ d :— $|$— :— $\|$

(iv) Ear-tests, in tune only, should now be given to the children in a variety of keys. Before each test it will be well to let the class sing the new *doh*.

STEP XXIV (STAFF)

(i) Modulator practice should be extended so as to introduce the other notes of the key of F.

(ii) The following or similar exercises, in tune only, should be written on the blackboard, and sung slowly by the class, to the Sol-fa names.

Example:—

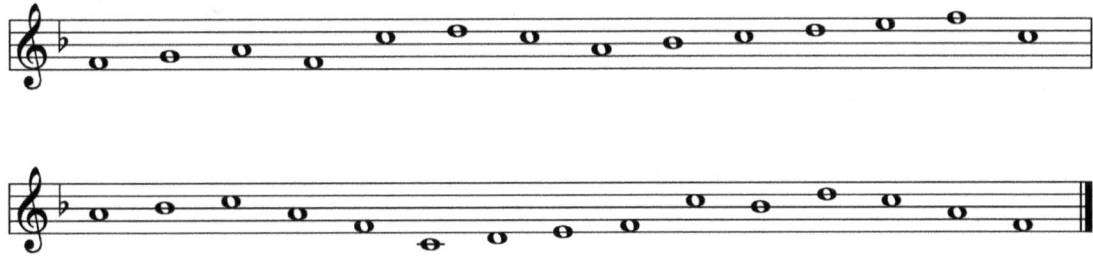

(iii) Exercises in Time and Tune.

(iv) Ear-tests of three notes, occasionally one with four notes (if it is an easy one) should be given to the children, and written down by them in the staff notation (in the key of C).

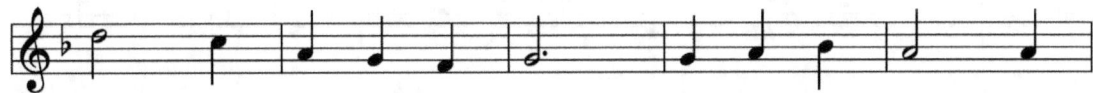

STEP XXV (Sol-fa)

Recapitulation of Steps XVII and XIX.

STEP XXVI (Staff)

Recapitulation of (i) and (ii) in Steps XVIII and XX introducing C♯ and F♮.

(iii) Exercises in Time and Tune.

(iv) The ear-tests should be given to the children, and written down by them in the key of G. It is most important that children should write with the new key signature.

STEP XXVII (Sol-fa)

Recapitulation of Steps XXI and XXIII.

STEP XXVIII (Staff)

Recapitulation of (i) and (ii) in Steps XXII and XXIV, introducing B♮ and E♭.

(iii) Exercises in Time and Tune.

(iv) The ear-tests should be given to the children, and written down by them in the key of F in the staff notation.

STEP XXIX (SOL-FA)

(i) Modulator practice in three keys, introducing various accidentals.

(ii) Easy exercises in Time and Tune introducing bridge-notes.

(iii) The class should be able by this time to write down ear-tests of four notes with tolerable ease.

STEP XXX (STAFF)

(i) Modulator practice in the keys of C, G, and F, introducing various accidentals.

(ii) Exercises in Time and Tune in the three keys.

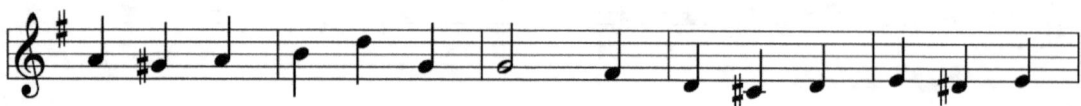

(iii) The class should be able to write down in the staff notation ear-tests of four notes in the three keys already learned.

STEP XXXI (SOL-FA)

(i) A short practice with the modulator, introducing various accidentals.

(ii) Exercises in Time and Tune, introducing bridge-notes.

(iii) Half-beat notes should be explained to the children in two-, three-, and four-beat measure.

(iv) The following or similar passages should be written on the blackboard, and sung to the syllable *doh*, both teacher and class beating time.

Examples:—

{| d :d | d.d:d.d| d :d.d| d :d.d|d.d:d | d.d:d | d.d:d.d| d :— ||

{| d :d :d | d .d:d .d :d | d :d :d .d| d :d .d :d }

{| d :d :d .d| d :d :d | d .d:d .d :d .d| d :d :— ||

{| d :d |d :d.d| d :d |d :d.d|d.d:d.d| d :d.d| d :d.d|d :—.d }

{| d :—.d|d :—.d| d :—.d|d :d | d :—.d|d.d:d.d| d :— |d :— ||

(v) A short rhythmic phrase on one note, introducing one or two half-beat notes, should be played two or three times.

Example:—

{| d   :d | d   :d .d | d .d :d .d | d   :— ||

(vi) The children should beat time while the teacher sings or plays the phrase; they should then sing it themselves, and when they can do this should write it down in their note-books.

STEP XXXII (STAFF)

(i) A short practice on the modulator in three keys, introducing various accidentals.

(ii) Quavers and dotted notes should be explained to the class.

(iii) The following or similar exercises should be written on the blackboard, and sung first to the time-names and afterwards to the syllable *doh*, both teacher and class beating time:—

Examples:—

(iv) Exercises in Time and Tune.

(v) A short rhythmic phrase on one note should be played or sung two or three times to the class. One or two quavers should be introduced, but no dotted notes.

Example:—

The children should beat time while the teacher sings or plays the phrase. They should then sing it themselves, and when they can do this, should write it down in the staff notation in their MS. books.

STEP XXXIII (SOL-FA)[6]

(i) Practice on the modulator, in the minor mode, introducing *se*, but the passage *f se l* should be avoided at first.

(ii) The following or similar exercises should be written on the blackboard, and sung slowly by the class.

> *Example:—*
>
> Lah is **A**.
>
> l   t   d'   t   l   se   l   m   f   m   l   t   l   se   l   m
>
> d   r   m   l   d'   t   l   m   f   l   m   l   t   se   l

(iii) Exercises 38, 39, 42, and 44 in the "Criterion Sight-Reader," Part III:—

> Lah is **F**.   M. 132.
>
> { | d :d | m :— | l₁ :l₁ | d :— | r :d | t₁ :d | r :f | m :— }
>
> { | m :m | r :— | d :d | t₁ :— | l₁ :m₁ | l₁ :d | t₁ :l₁ | l₁ :— ||

> Lah is **G**.   M. 132.
>
> { | l₁ :m₁ | l₁ :m₁ | l₁ :d | m :— | r :t₁ | d :l₁ | d :l₁ | t₁ :— }
>
> { | l₁ :d | l₁ :d | l₁ :d | m₁ :— | f₁ :f₁ | m₁ :l₁ | d :t₁ | l₁ :— ||

> Lah is **D**.
>
> { | m :f :m | l :— :m | d :— :r | m :— :— | l₁ :— :t₁ | d :r :m }
>
> { | r :— :d | t₁ :— :— | m :f :m | l :— :m | d :— :r | r :m :— }
>
> { | l₁ :t₁ :f | m :— :r | t₁ :— :d | l₁ :— :— ||

> Lah is **E**.   M. 108.
>
> { | l₁ :t₁ :d | t₁ :— :l₁ | m :— :— | m :— :— | f :m :r }
>
> { | d :t₁ :l₁ | r :— :— | r :— :— | d :t₁ :l₁ | t₁ :— :d }
>
> { | l₁ :— :— | l :— :— | m :r :f | m :d :t₁ | l₁ :— :— ||

---

[6]If the Tonic Minor method is adopted, the teacher should omit Steps XXXIII to XL, and take them, as set out in Appendix III, *after Step L*. On no account should *both* methods be taught.

The class should at first sing the tune only, without the time, if the teacher considers it advisable.

(iv) Easy ear-tests in the minor mode.

Examples:—

D *minor.*

d¹ l se l   l se l d¹   m l se l   m d m l   l t l se

STEP XXXIV (STAFF)

(i) The modulator should now be drawn so as to bring the notes of the minor key into prominence. This may be done as in the illustration:—

The teacher should only point to the *right* of the chord of A minor when he wishes to indicate G♯.

(ii) The following or similar exercises in tune only should be written on the blackboard, and sung slowly by the class.

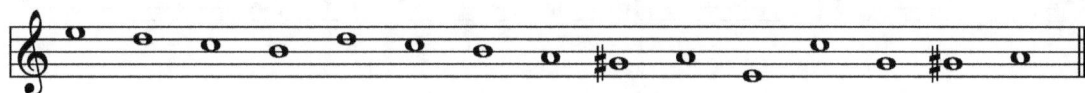

(iii) Exercises in the Minor Key:—

(iv) Ear-tests in A minor should be given to the class and written down by them in the staff notation.

STEP XXXV (SOL-FA)

(i) Practice on the modulator, in the minor mode, introducing *ba se lah*, and *fah se lah*.

(ii) The following and similar exercises should be written on the blackboard, and sung slowly by the class.

Example:—

Lah is **G**.

l   m   d¹   t   l   s   f   m   m   se   l   m   ba   se   l   d¹

t   l   m   l   s   f   m   d   r   m   f   se   l   se   l

(iii) Exercises in Time and Tune (48, 52, 55, and 60, in the "Criterion Sight Reader," Part III).

Lah is **F**.   M. 126.

{ :m₁ | m :— | — :m₁ | m :— | — :m₁ | m :m | r :f | m :— | — :r }

{ | d :m | d :— | t₁ :r | t₁ :— | l₁ :d | t₁ :— | l₁ :— | — || }

Lah is **D**.   M. 104.

{ | l :— :l₁ | l :— :l₁ | l :s :f | m :— :r | d :t₁ :l₁ | t₁ :d :t₁ }

{ | l₁ :— :— | m :— :— | l :— :— | m :— :— | l₁ :— :— || }

Lah is **C**.   M. 96.

{ | m :l₁ | d :— | l :m | l :d¹ | t :l | m :d | m :l | m :— }

{ | m :l | d :m | l₁ :m | f :m | l :l₁ | d :m | l :d | m :— || }

Lah is **C**.   M. 100.

{ | l :l | m :m | d :d | l₁ :— | t₁ :t₁ | d :r | m :f | m :— }

{ | l :l | m :m | d :d | l₁ :— | t₁ :d | r :m | f :m | l₁ :— || }

(iv) Ear-tests in the minor mode should be sung or played to the children, and written down by them in their note-books.

Examples:—

A *minor*.

l   se   l   d¹   d   m   l   se   se   l   d¹   t   se   l   f   m   l   se   t   l

STEP XXXVI (STAFF)

(i) Practice on the modulator, in the key of A minor, introducing F, G♯, A, and F♯, G♯, A. Explain the two forms of minor scale, and make the class sing them to the Sol-fa names.

(ii) Exercises in the Minor Key:—

(iii) Ear-tests, introducing the new notes learned, should be played or sung to the class, and written down by the children in the staff notation in the key of A minor.

STEP XXXVII (Sol-fa)

(i) Modulator practice in the minor mode.

(ii) Exercises 8, 9, 18, 19, and 22 in the "Criterion Sight Reader," Part IV:—

KEY **D**. M. 116.

$\{\|$d :-.s₁|r :s₁ |d.r:m.f|s :m |d¹ :l |l,,s:m.d|r :— |— :-. $\}$

$\{\|$d :s₁ |r :s₁ |d.r:m.f|s :d¹ |d¹ :fe.l|s :r.m|d :— |— : $\}$

$\{\|$r.r:d.r|m :m |f.f:m.f|l :s |f.f:r.r|s :m |d :t₁.d|r :— $\}$

$\{\|$r.r:d.r|m :m |f.f:m.f|l :s |d¹ :t.l|s :f |m :r |s :— $\}$

$\{\|$d :s₁ |r :s₁ |d.r:m.f|s :m |d¹ :l |l,,s:m,,d|r :— |— :— $\}$

$\{\|$d :s₁ |r :s₁ |d.r:m.f|s :d¹ |d¹ :fe.l|s. :r.m|d. :s₁.s₁|d.r:m.f$\}$

$\{\|$s :— |— : |d. :s₁.s₁|d.r:m.f|s :— |— : |s :— |— : $\}$

$\{\|$l :— |— : |t :— |— : |d¹ :— |— : $\|\|$

KEY **G**. M. 100.

$\{\|$s :f :m,,r.m,,f|s :f :m,,r.m,,f|s .f :m .f :m ,,r$\}$

$\{\|$d :t₁ :s₁,l₁.t₁,d|r .s :m :s₁,l₁.t₁,d|r .s :m :d,r.m,f$\}$

$\{\|$s :f .m :r ,,d|d :t₁ .d,r:m .f |s :f :m,,r.m,,f$\}$

$\{\|$s :f :m,,r.m,,f|s .f :m .f :m ,,r|d :t₁ : .t₁ $\}$

$\{\|$d,r.m,f:s .m :r |d,r.m,f:s .m :r |d,r.m,f :s .s :s .s $\}$

{ | s₁.l.s,f:m .s :m .d | t₁,d.r,d:t₁   :l₁ | l₁,t₁.d,t₁:l₁   :s₁   }

{ | l₁,t₁.d,r:m   :m | m .f :m .r :d .t₁ | l₁,t₁.d,r:m   :m   }

{ | m .f :m .r :d .t₁ | d .t₁ :d .r :m .f | s   :f   :m,r.m,f }

{ | s   :f   :m,r.m,f | s .f :m .f :m   .,r | d   :t₁   :s₁.l₁,t₁,d }

{ | r .s :m   :s₁,l₁.t₁,d| r .s :m   :d,r.m,f| s   :s₁.s₁:l₁.,t₁| t₁   :d   :— || }

Lah is **E**.   M. 144.

{ | d   :l₁   :— | d.t₁:d.r:m | r .d:t₁ :t₁.l₁| se₁ :— :t₁ | d   :l₁   :— }

{ | d.t₁:d .r:m | r.d :t₁ :d.t₁| l₁ :— : | r .d:r.m:f .m| r   :— :t₁ }

{ | r.d :t₁.d:r.m| d   :—.t₁:l₁ | f .m:r.d:t₁ | m .r:d.t₁:l₁.d| t₁.l₁:se₁ :—.l₁ }

{ | l₁ :— : | d.t₁:d.t₁:d.r| m   :— :d | r .d:r.d:r .m| f   :—.m:r }

{ | d   :m   :— | d   :m   :— | l₁,t₁:l₁.t₁:d.l₁| t₁.d:t₁   :—.l₁| l₁   :— :— || }

KEY **G**.   M. 126.

{ | s   :f .m:r.,m| f   :—.m:r.,d| m   :— : | :d.l₁:t₁.d| r   :s₁   : .f }

{ | m   :—.r:d.,r| s₁   :— : | .s₁:l₁.s₁:t₁.,d| m   :r : | .s₁:l₁.s₁:t₁.d }

{ | m.,r:d : | s₁.,s₁:s₁.l₁:l₁.,s₁| s₁   :   : | s₁   :s₁.,s₁:s₁.,l₁| s₁   :— :   }

{ | :.s₁:l₁.t₁| d.,t₁:r :— | :s₁.l₁:t₁.d| r   :s₁   :s |— :f .m:r.,m }

{ | f   :   : .m| m   :—.r:d.,r| m   :— : | .s₁:l₁.t₁:m.,r| r   :d : || }

Lah is C.

{| d :r :m | l₁ :— :— | l₁ :— :— | d :r :m | l :— :— }

{| l :— :— | l :s :f | m :l :se | l :t :l | se :— :— }

{| l :m :f | m :— :— | l :— :— | l :d :r | m :— :— }

{| l :— :— | l :l₁ :l | se :l :m | d :r :m | l₁ :— :— ||}

(iii) The class should practise writing out well-known tunes, in easy time (such as "God save the King"). Time and tune together should not at first be attempted. The notes of a tune might be written one day and put into the proper time the next.

STEP XXXVIII (STAFF)

(i) Modulator practice in the key of A minor.

(ii) Exercises from the "Simplex Music Reader," to be selected by the teacher, for practising the class in any points in which he thinks they are specially deficient.

(iii) Exercises in the Minor Key:—

(iv) The class should continue to practise writing out well-known tunes in easy time. Time and tune together should not be attempted at first. As already stated, the notes of a tune might be written one day and put into proper time the next.

From this point onward the staff notation only need be used; but any difficulties which arise can generally be explained to the class by means of the Sol-fa notation. As soon as the class is able to sing fairly easily in any key, using the Sol-fa names, these should be dropped and the syllable *laa* substituted. The teacher must use his own discretion in each case, as no positive rule can be made: the proficiency of the children must be the sole guide.

STEP XXXIX

(i) Practice on the modulator in the key of E minor (See Step XXXIV), introducing both forms of the minor scale.

(ii) The following and similar exercises should be written on the blackboard, and sung slowly by the class:—

Example:—

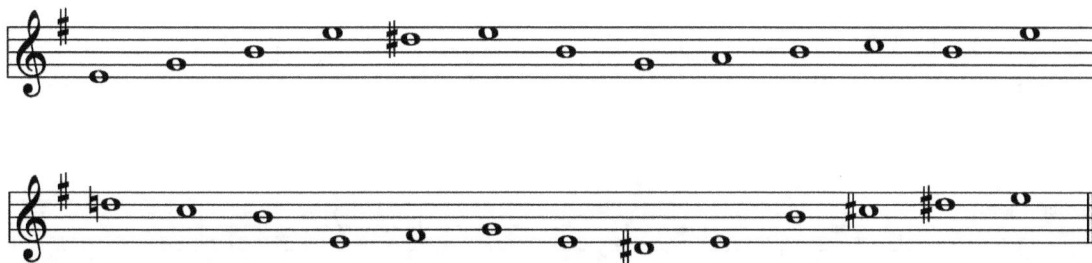

(iii) Exercises in E minor.

(iv) Four or eight bars of a well-known tune to be written out by the children in staff notation.

STEP XL

(i) Practice on the modulator in the key of D minor (see Step XXXIV, i), introducing both forms of the minor scale.

(ii) The following and similar exercises should be written on the blackboard, and sung slowly by the class.

Example:—

(iii) Exercises in D minor.

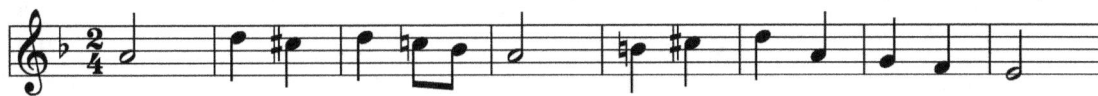

(iv) Four or eight bars of a well-known tune to be written out by the class in
   the staff notation.

STEP XLI

(i) Practice on the modulator in the key of D. The modulator should now be extended so as to include the new key; and transitions from D to G may with advantage be introduced. Only easy intervals should be practised at first.

(ii) The following and similar exercises should be written on the blackboard, and sung slowly by the class.

Example:—

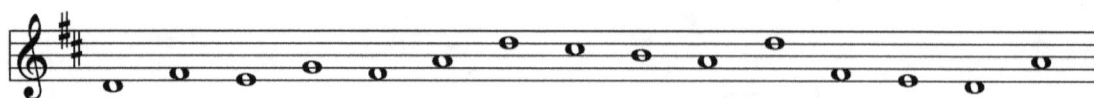

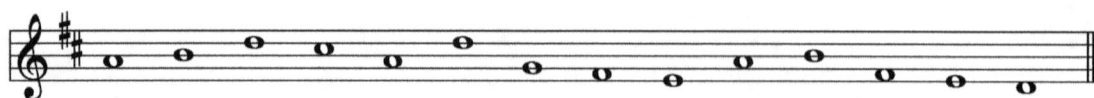

(iii) Exercises in D major.

(iv) Easy ear-tests should be played or sung, and written down by the children in the key of D.

STEP XLII

(i) Practice on the modulator introducing more difficult intervals in the key of D, also G♯ and D♮.

(ii) The following and similar exercises should be written on the blackboard, and sung slowly by the class:—

Example:—

(iii) Exercises in D, including *fe* and *ta*.

(iv) Ear-tests, including G♯ and C♮, should be sung or played to the class, and written down in the key of D.

Examples:—

STEP XLIII

(i) Practice on the modulator in the key of B♭. The modulator should now be extended to the left, so as to include the new key; and transition from B♭ to F may with advantage be introduced. Only easy intervals should be practised at first.

(ii) The following and similar exercises should be written out on the blackboard, and sung slowly by the class:—

Example:—

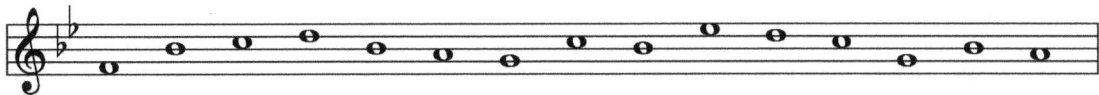

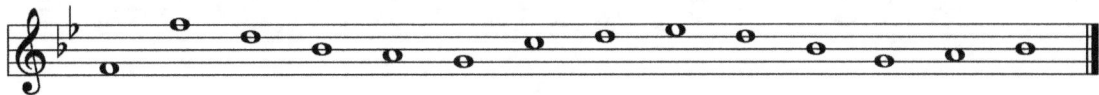

(iii) Exercises in B♭.

(iv) Easy ear-tests should be played or sung, and written down by the children in the key of B♭.

Examples:—

STEP XLIV

(i) Practice on the modulator, introducing more difficult intervals in the key of B♭, also E♮ and A♭.

(ii) The following and similar exercises should be written on the blackboard, and sung slowly by the children:—

Example:—

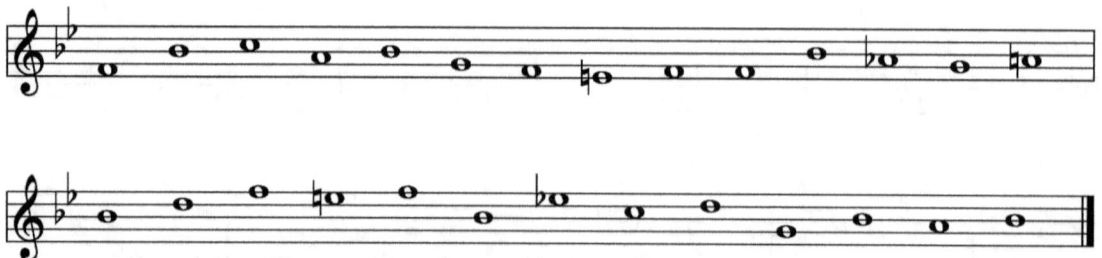

(iii) Exercises in B♭ including *fe* and *ta*.

(iv) Ear-tests, including E♮ and A♭, should be played or sung to the class, and written down by them in B♭.

Examples:—

STEP XLV

(i) Practice on the modulator in the key of A. The modulator should be extended to the right so as to include the new key; and transition from A to D may with advantage be introduced. Only easy intervals should be practised at first.

(ii) The following and similar exercises should be written on the blackboard, and sung slowly by the class:—

Example:—

(iii) Exercises in A.

(iv) Easy ear-tests should be played or sung, and written down by the children in the key of A.

Examples:—

STEP XLVI

(i) Practice on the modulator in the key of A, introducing more difficult intervals, including D♯ and G♮.

(ii) The following and similar exercises should be written on the blackboard, and sung slowly by the class:—

Example:—

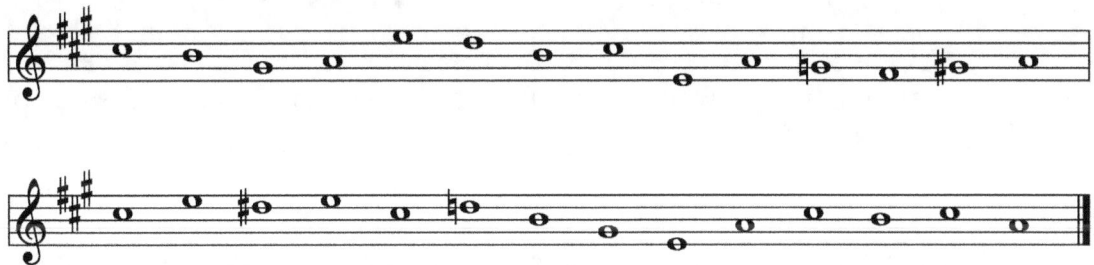

(iii) Examples in A, including *fe* and *ta*.

(iv) Four or eight bars of a well-known tune to be written down in the key of A by the class.

STEP XLVII

(i) Practice on the modulator in the key of E♭. The modulator should be extended to the left so as to include the new key; and transitions from E♭ to B♭ may with advantage be introduced. Only easy intervals should be practised at first.

(ii) The following and similar exercises should be written on the blackboard, and sung slowly by the class.

Example:—

(iii) Exercises in E♭.

(iv) Easy ear-tests should be played or sung, and written down by the children in the key of E♭.

Examples:—

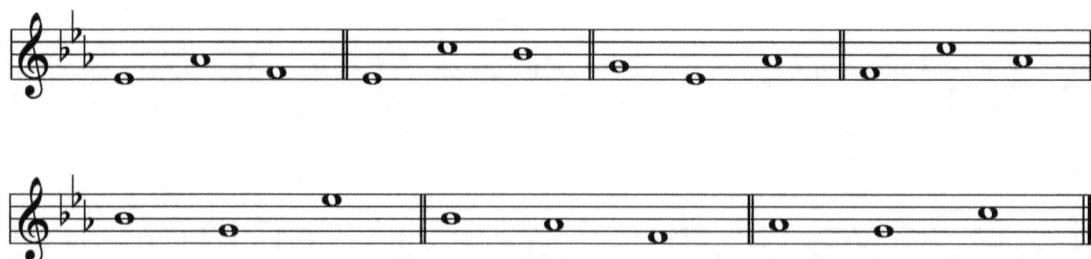

STEP XLVIII

(i) Practice on the modulator in the key of E♭, introducing more difficult intervals, including A♮ and D♭.

(ii) The following and similar exercises should be written on the blackboard, and sung slowly by the class.

(iii) Exercises in E♭, including *fe* and *ta*.

(iv) Four or eight bars of a well-known tune should be written down by the class.

STEP XLIX

(i) Compound duple time should be explained to the children, and well-known tunes sung by them (*e.g.*, "Come, lasses and lads"). Time (two beats in each bar) should be beaten by both teacher and class.

(ii) The following or similar exercises should be written on the blackboard, and sung by the children, who should also beat time.

Example:—

(iii) Exercises in 6/8 time.

(iv) Ear-tests should consist of short phrases in Time and Tune, which the children should first learn to sing by heart to the syllable *laa*, and then write down.

Example:—

or,

STEP L

(i) The semiquaver and dotted quaver should be explained to the class.

(ii) The following and similar exercises should be written on the blackboard, and sung, both teacher and class beating time.

By removing the alternate bar marks the phrase can be changed into $\frac{4}{4}$ time, and the class should sing it beating 4 in a bar.

(iii) Exercises in dotted quaver.

(iv) Ear-tests as in Step XLIX.

A few keys and times only remain to be learned; but it is unnecessary to indicate further the methods or order in which these should be taught. The children should be able to sing moderately difficult passages in C, D, E♭, F, G, A, and B♭, and the difficulty of adjusting themselves to these tonics with different signatures is not great. For instance, if they can sing in E♭ with the Tonic Sol-fa names, they will find, when they know the signatures, that E with four sharps is just as easy. Many small points are sure to arise incidentally during the lessons which must be left to the teacher to deal with; for it is manifestly impossible in a book of this size and nature to provide for every contingency, or to predict the questions arising from the ingenuity of the juvenile mind.

In the Student's book of exercises will be found a large number of tunes in all major keys for purposes of revision. [It is advisable to work through these before teaching the Tonic Minor.]

APPENDIX I

A Table of Hand Signs (with Illustrations)

NOTE.—*The diagrams show the hand as seen from the left of the teacher, not as seen from the front. Teachers should particularly notice this.*

SOH.
The GRAND or *bright* tone.

TE.
The PIERCING or *sensitive* tone.

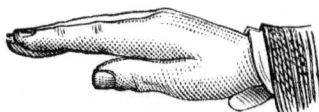

ME.
The STEADY or *calm* tone.

DOH.
The STRONG or *firm* tone.

RAY.
The ROUSING or *hopeful* tone.

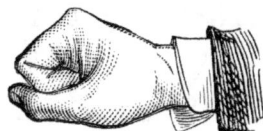

LAH.
The SAD or *weeping* tone.

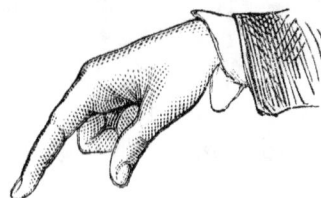

FAH.
The DESOLATE or *awe-inspiring* tone.

NOTE. —These proximate verbal descriptions of mental effect are only true of the tones of the scale when sung slowly—when the ear is filled with the key, and when the effect is not modified by harmony.

For *Fe*, let the teacher point his first finger horizontally to the left. For *Ta*, ditto to the right. To the class these positions will be reversed, and will correspond with the Modulator. For *Se* let the teacher point his forefinger straight towards the class.

APPENDIX II

TIME NAMES

This book was originally intended for teachers who had learned the Sol-fa Notation, in order to give them a method for connecting the two notations from the beginning. But the book has been so widely taken up by those to whom Sol-fa is unfamiliar, that, in response to many requests, certain essentials of that notation are now included, viz., the Hand-signs and the Time-names—the latter with instructions as to the Steps in the book when they should be used.

It is impossible to overrate the immense value of these names in the teaching of time; for the system is not based upon an intellectual arithmetical learning of time and accent, but upon the sense impression given by the pattering sound of certain monosyllabic names for notes of different value, the combined sound of which reproduces the pattern of the music.

(i) A note occupying a single beat is called *taa*, whatever the length of the beat may be:—Thus in $\frac{2}{4}$ time each crotchet is *taa*. In $\frac{3}{4}$ time each crotchet is *taa*. In $\frac{2}{2}$ time each minim is *taa*. In $\frac{6}{8}$ time each dotted crotchet is *taa*.

(ii) If a note is prolonged beyond the length of a beat (*e.g.*, dotted, tied, or doubled), the consonant is dropped and the next beat is called *aa*. Thus:—

(iii) When a beat is divided into two equal parts the time-name is *taatai* (pronounced *taatay*). Thus in times where each beat is a minim, two crotchets, forming together a complete beat, are called *taatai*; and, in the same way, when each beat is worth a crotchet, two quavers, forming together a complete beat, are also called *taatai*.

[7]The rests of different length are made by substituting the letter *s* for the letter *t;*
e.g., beat rest = *saa*, half-beat rest = *sai*, and so on.

taa   taa   taa   taatai   taatai   taatai   taa - aa   taatai   taa - aa - aa

The same time-names would also be used for the following:—

Examples of dotted beats:—

taa - aatai   taa - aatai   taa - aatai taa   taa   taa-aatai

(iv) When a beat is divided into four notes of equal length the time-names are *tafatefe*.

ta fa te fe taa   ta fa te fe   taa ta fa te fe taa

In the same way a half and two quarters are called *taatefe*, while for two quarters followed by a half-beat the time-names are *tafatai*

(vi) For any beat divided into three equal notes the time-names are *taataitee*. (These names apply both to triplets and to the natural subdivision of a compound beat.)

APPENDIX III

There has always been a difference of opinion between orthodox Sol-faists and advocates of the Staff Notation regarding the treatment of the minor scale; and the Sol-fa treatment of it has probably been one of the reasons why many musicians have been unwilling to adopt the system as a whole. The Tonic Sol-faist treats the minor scale as merely the relative to its major; while the large majority of musicians treat the minor scale as a self-existent scale with its own tonic, etc., obeying its own laws which, in most respects, are the same as those of the major scale.

The late Dr. Sawyer's Sight-reading book, embodying this view, while at the same time using many of the excellences of the Tonic Sol-fa system, is well known to most teachers, and has been used at many of the best-known institutions for many years. There is therefore nothing new in the alternative system advocated in this Appendix, which has been added in response to requests from teachers who find the book useful, but who dissent from the Sol-fa treatment of the minor scale.

There is one obvious advantage in the Sol-fa treatment of the minor for those students who are not likely to proceed to instrumental work; for, if the minor tune does not modulate beyond the relative major, the key, so far as the syllables are concerned, does not change. From a musical point of view, however, it is a distinct disadvantage that singers should be unaware that a modulation has taken place; and this is likely to be the case with all but the specially gifted.

Again, through the adoption of the relative instead of the tonic minor the whole case for "mental effects" (the basis of the Tonic Sol-fa method) is to a large extent stultified. The Tonic, instead of being the *firm* note, is merely the *sad* note (*lah* of the major scale); the third note of the scale, instead of being the *calm* note, becomes the *firm* note (*i.e.*, the real tonic of the key); while the fifth note of the scale, instead of being the *bright* note, becomes the *calm* note, and its special *dominating* character is denied by the "mental effect" given to it. The difficulty of adjusting the ideas to these new "mental effects" is shown in various ways by the pupils; one of the most usual being an almost irresistible inclination to sing *doh* for *lah*; especially when it is taken by skip, in reality, a most natural and musical mistake to make.

In teaching the tonic minor it is advisable to let the class look through the tune before singing it, and point out any modulation to the relative major, and the place where it returns to the original key. The singing of such tunes with Sol-fa names sometimes entails the use of bridge-notes (which do not tend to simplicity), and it is therefore recommended that children should, as soon as possible, sing the minor tunes to the syllable *laa*. The great advantage of this treatment of the minor key is that children realise from the first that the Tonic in the minor is *doh* just as it is in the major, and this is a knowledge that will be of great service to them in their instrumental work, and especially so in transposition.

The "mental effects" are now the same in both major and minor keys.

MAJOR.	MENTAL EFFECT.	MINOR.
Doh'	Firm.	Doh'
Te	Piercing	Te
Lah	Sad	La (pronounced "law")
Soh	Bright	Soh
Fah	Desolate	Fah
Me	Calm	Ma (pronounced "maw")
Ray	Rousing	Ray
Doh	Firm	Doh

In the ascending minor scale (melodic form) the sixth note becomes *lah* (as in the major).

As in the case of the major keys, C major was taken first; so in the minor keys, it is best to take C minor first.

In the following Steps the Sol-fa tunes have been translated into the tonic minor, or new ones substituted.

In order that children may learn to find the right signatures of the minor scales, it is a good plan (after discussing with them the places where the semitones occur as compared with their position in the major scale) to write up on the blackboard the two forms of the minor scale in (say) C minor, and get the children to say which signature would be most likely to fit them. They will soon see that the signature of three flats comes nearest to what they want. Another scale might be written up for them, *e.g.*, E minor, and they will soon find one sharp as the signature. Other examples might be given.

STEP XXXIII (Sol-fa)

(i) Practise on the modulator in the minor key, taking *Doh* as the tonic, using *ma* instead of *me*, and *la* instead of *lah*. The passage *la to doh*[1] should be avoided at first.

(ii) The following or similar exercises should be written on the blackboard, and sung slowly by the class.

Example:—

d   r   ma r   d   ma s   la s   d¹ t   d¹ s   la s   d¹ s   la s   f   la s   f   ma r   d

(iii) Exercises in time and tune.

F minor.

| ma :ma | s :— | d :d | ma :— | f :ma | r :ma | f :la | s :— |

| s :s | f :— | ma :ma | r :— | d :s | d :ma | r :d | d :— ‖

G minor.

| d :s₁ | d :s₁ | d :ma | s :— | f :r | ma :d | ma :d | r :— |

| d :ma | d :ma | d :ma | s₁ :— | la₁ :la₁ | s₁ :d | ma :r | d :— ‖

D minor.

| s :la :s | d¹ :— :s | ma :— :f | s :— :— | d :— :r |

| ma :f :s | f :— :ma | r :— :— | s :la :s | d¹ :— :s |

| ma :— :f | f :s :— | d :r :la | s :— :f | r :— :ma | d :— :— ‖

E minor.

| d :r :ma | r :— :d | s :— :— | s :— :— | la :s :f |

| ma :r :d | f :— :— | f :— :— | ma :r :d | r :— :ma |

| d :— :— | d :— :— | s :f :la | s :ma :r | d :— :ma | d :— :— ‖

The class should at first sing the tune only, without the time, if the teacher considers it advisable.

(iv) Easy ear-tests in the minor key should be given to the children, and written down by them in their note-books.

Examples:—

D *minor.*

ma d t, d   d t, d ma   s d¹ t d¹   s ma s d¹   s la s d¹

STEP XXXIV (STAFF)

(i) The following or similar exercises should be written on the blackboard, and sung slowly by the children (C or C♯ minor).

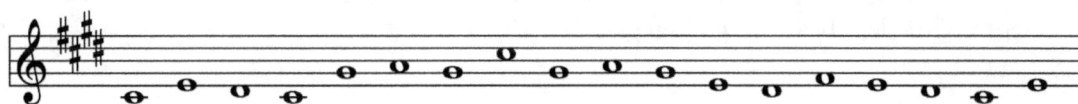

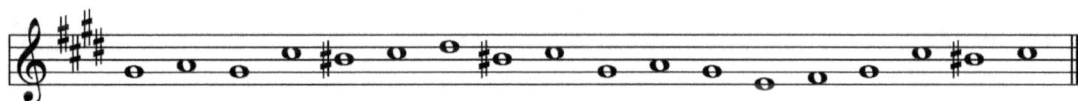

(ii) Exercises in time and tune in C minor and C♯ minor.

(iii) Ear-tests, introducing the new notes learned, should be sung or played to the children, and written down by them in the Staff Notation in the key of C minor or C♯ minor.

STEP XXXV (Sol-fa)

(i) Practise on the modulator in the minor key, introducing *s l t d¹* and *d¹ ta la s* (the melodic minor scale).

(ii) The following or similar passages should be written out on the blackboard, and sung slowly by the class:—

Example:—

D *minor.*

d ma r d s l t d¹ d¹ ta la s d¹ ta la s s l t d¹ s la s ma r d

(iii) Exercises in time and tune:—

F *minor.*

{ :s₁ | s :— |— :s₁ | s :— |— :s₁ | s :s | f :la | s :— |— :f }
{ | ma :s | ma :— | r :f | r :— | d :ma | r :— | d :— |— ‖

D *minor.*

{ | d :— :d¹ | d¹ :ta :la | s :— :ma | s :l :t }
{ | d¹ :— :s | la :s :ma | d :ma :r | d :— :— ‖

C *minor.*

{ | d :ma | s :— | ma :s | d¹ :— | s :l | t :d¹ | ta :la | s :— }
{ | la :s | d¹ :s | f :la | s :ma | d :s | l :t | d¹ :— | d :— ‖

C minor.

{| d¹ :ta :l | s :— :— | la :s :f | ma :— :— | f :ma :r }

{| d :ma :s | l :t :d¹ | t :— :— | r¹ :d¹ :t | d¹ :— :s }

{| la :f :la | s :— :— | s :l :t | d¹ :ta :la | s :— :ma | d :— :— ||}

(iv) Ear-tests in the minor key should be sung or played to the children, and written down by them in their note-books.

Example:—

A minor.

d t₁ d ma   ma₁ s₁ d t₁   t₁ d ma r   t₁ d la s   d ta₁ la₁ s₁

STEP XXXVI (STAFF)

(i) Explain once more the two forms of the minor scale, and make the class sing them to the Sol-fa syllables.

(ii) The following or similar passages should be written on the blackboard, and sung slowly by the class (C minor and C♯ minor).

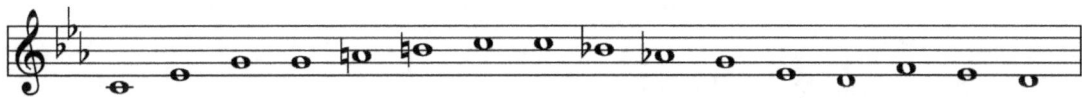

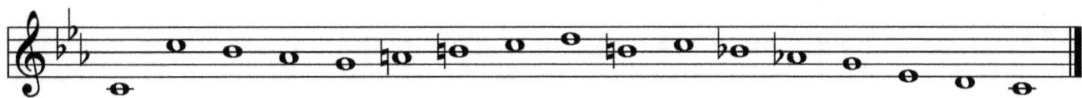

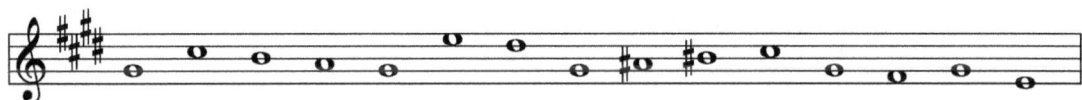

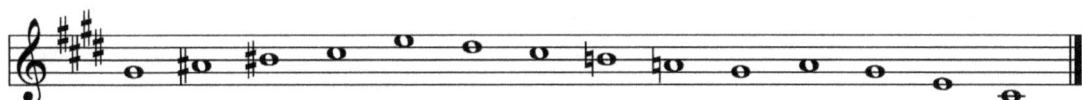

(iii) Exercises in time and tune in C minor and C♯ minor.

(iv) Ear-tests, introducing the new notes learned, should be sung or played to the children, and written down by them in the Staff Notation in the key of C minor or C♯ minor.

STEP XXXVII (Sol-fa)

(i) Modulator practice in the minor key.

(ii) Exercises in time and tune:—

C minor.

```
{ | s  :l.t |d' :ta.la | s  :d.ma | r  :d  | la :s.f | s  :d'.s | la.s:f.ma | ma :r  }
{ | f  :la.f | s  :d.ma | la :d'.la | s  :f  | ma.r:d.r | ma.s:l.t | d' :s.ma | d  :—  ||
```

G minor.

```
{ | d  :ma.r:d.t, | d  :s  :s  | la :s  :f  | s  :—.ma:d | d  :ta, :la,  }
{ | s, :—.l,:t,.d | r  :ma :d  | s  :— :—   | s  :r.ma:f | ma :r.ma:d  }
{ |d.ta,:la,,s,:l,.t,|d.ma:s  :s  |la.f:ma :r | d  :s :d.ma|ma.r:d :t, | d :—:— ||
```

E minor.

{| ma :d :— | ma.r:ma.f:s | f.ma:r :r.d | t₁ :— :r | ma :d :— }

{| ma.r:ma.f:s | f.ma:r :ma.r | d :— : | s :l.t :d¹ | d¹ :ta.la:s }

{| ᵗᵃs :f.m :r.m | d :— : | ᵐs :l.t :d¹ | d¹ :ta.la:s | ma :f.s :la }

{| la :s.f :ma | s :f.ma:r.ma | d :s :— | f.la:s.ma:r.ma | d :— :— ||

(iii) The class should begin to practise writing out well-known tunes in easy time (such as "A north country maid"). Time and tune together need not be attempted at first. The notes of the tune might be written out one day, and put into proper time the next.

STEP XXXVIII (STAFF)

(i) Exercises in time and tune, introducing modulation to the relative major. This may be practised on a modulator which introduces both minor and relative major keys side by side. The best bridge-notes are (where possible) *soh* (minor), changing to *me* in the relative major; and *ma* changing to *doh* in the relative major, and *vice versa*. The first note is very often *ta* (changing to *soh*); for *ta* may mean merely the descending melodic minor, or it may mean a modulation into the relative major.

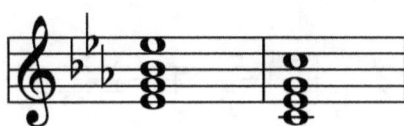

(ii) Exercises in time and tune in C minor and C♯ minor. (The notes which should be bridge-notes are marked with a star).

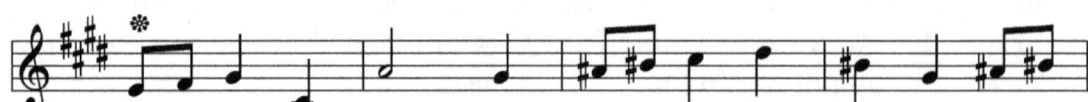

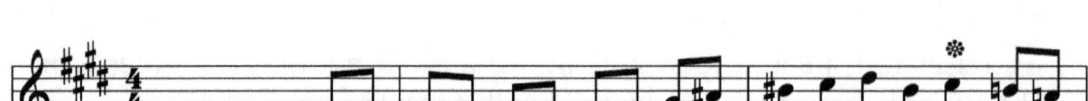

(iii) The class should continue to practise the writing out of well-known tunes, following the recommendation in Step XXXVII (iii).

STEP XXXIX

(i) The following or similar passages should be written on the blackboard, and sung slowly by the class. Key G minor and G♯ minor.

(ii) Exercises in time and tune in G minor and G♯ minor.

(iii) Four or eight bars of a well-known tune to be written out by the children in the Staff Notation in the key of G minor or G♯ minor.

STEP XL

(i) The following and similar passages should be written out on the blackboard, and sung slowly by the class (F minor and F♯ minor).

(ii) Exercises in time and tune in the keys of F minor and F♯ minor.

(iii) Ear-tests as in the last Step.